MEET my FAMiLY!

FOR MY SISTER GAIL, A LOVING PART OF MY OWN JUST-RIGHT FAMILY —L.P.S.

FOR GRAMS —S.F.C.

Millbrook Press
A division of Lerner Publishing Group, Inc.
241 First Avenue North
Minneapolis, MN 55401 USA

For reading levels and more information, look up this title at
www.lernerbooks.com.

Designed by Lindsey Owens.
Main body text set in ITC Avant Garde Gothic 12/18.
Typeface provided by Adobe Systems.
The illustrations in this book were painted digitally in Photoshop.

Library of Congress Cataloging-in-Publication Data

Names: Salas, Laura Purdie. | Coleman, Stephanie Fizer, illustrator.
Title: Meet my family! : animal babies and their families / Laura Purdie
    Salas ; illustrated by Stephanie Fizer Coleman.
Other titles: Animal babies and their families
Description: Minneapolis : Millbrook Press, (2018) | Audience: Age
    5–9. | Audience: K to grade 3. | Includes bibliographical references.
Identifiers: LCCN 2017020219 (print) | LCCN 2017021030 (ebook) |
    ISBN 9781512498639 (eb pdf) | ISBN 9781512425321 (lb : alk. paper)
Subjects: LCSH: Animals—Infancy—Juvenile literature.
Classification: LCC QL763 (ebook) | LCC QL763 .S25 2018 (print) |
    DDC 591.3/92—dc23

LC record available at https://lccn.loc.gov/2017020219

Manufactured in the United States of America
1-41286-23245-7/17/2017

MEET my FAMiLY!

ANIMAL BABIES AND THEIR FAMILIES

LAURA PURDIE SALAS

illustrated by

STEPHANIE
FIZER COLEMAN

Millbrook Press / Minneapolis

My parents both take care of me.

My mother and father stay close to our nest. They keep me and my brothers and sisters safe from foxes and other hungry creatures! They also teach us to find tasty grains.

tundra swan cygnet

I've never met my dad.

My dad's not part of *my* family. He's never even seen me! He lives off by himself somewhere, and I live with my mom in our den.

raccoon kit

I'm the only kid around.

I wish I had a brother or sister my age. Having Mum all to myself is great, but I sure would like someone to chase and race with.

horse foal

That doesn't sound so bad!

You are soooo lucky! I have to climb over all my brothers and sisters just to get to dinner.

piglet

I'm in charge of all my meals.

I find my own food below sunny skies.
I graze for grasses and plants, just like
Amai and Baba and all the elders do.

white rhino calf

Mi madre brings me lunch.

I spend all day in my nest. When I was very small, mis padres used to throw up entire fish into my mouth. Now I grab that fish right out of their bills!

wood stork chick

We've lived one place since I was born.

I've lived in my family lodge for almost two years. When walls need fixing, I hunt for sticks. Yippee! I paddle and nibble and gnaw. Then I drag a stick back and poke it in place. Soon I'll build my own lodge.

beaver kit

orangutan infant

We move around a bunch.

Each night, my ibu builds us a new nest high in the branches of a tree. I never know where I'll be, but I always know she'll be right beside me.

Ladies all look after me.

My mama takes care of me. But my grandma, my aunties, and wakina mama wote in the herd also care for me. No boys are allowed here, except for calves like me. When I'm all grown up, I will live on my own.

elephant calf

Dad holds me till first light.

Mamãe only comes at dinner time, but Papai stays nearby always. I sleep snuggled up on him, and his hair is like a thick, warm blanket.

South American
titi monkey infant

My family frolics in a group.

My family loves to play! We slip and slide and swim together. I chase my ma and my brothers and sisters on slippery river slopes. Tag, you're it!

North American river otter pup

I'm solo, day and night.

When I hatched from my egg, many other hatchlings crowded the sandy beach. We hurried toward the water and were swept away in swirling waves. Now I swim alone in the silent ocean.

green sea turtle hatchling

I look just like my parents.

I already looked like my mom when I was born—only smaller. I swam off on my own right away to hunt for food. I'm fierce, and I'm growing. I don't need *anybody* to take care of me!

great white shark pup

We sure don't look the same!

Can you believe I wasn't even round when I hatched? I was a larva, long and prickly. Now that I'm a pupa, my body has ridges instead of prickles. After my next change, I'll be round and plump and polka-dotted like my parents. Finally!

ladybug pupa

Look! My dad gives piggybacks.

I don't look like my parents either. But check this out! Mi p'pa gives me a ride to my very own pond. I slide off his back and glide right in. I'll swim here until my arms and legs are fully grown.

poison dart frog tadpole

We play a wrestling game.

I'm the only pup in the pack. All the big
wolves help take care of me! Sometimes,
my pop—*hey!*—wrestles with me.
I—*oops*—even—*oof*—win sometimes.
And he does NOT let me win!

wolf pup

Twice the moms— that's what I have.

Lots of chicks have a mom and dad, but some of us have two mākuahine instead. One stays with me at the nest, and the other flies off to find food in the warm waves. Then they switch. We are family: chick, parents, and love.

Laysan albatross chick

Two dads are what I've got!

My two daddies feed me fish. One is always next to me, strong and sturdy and warm. Both of them protect me and play with me. I am double-daddy lucky.

chinstrap penguin chick

Someone else gave birth to me.

Guddi adopted me! She is not a monkey like me. She barks instead of squeaks, but that's OK. I run to her and hold tight to her long white fur. She feeds me and lets me ride under her belly.

dog and rhesus macaque infant

harbor seal pup

My mother works a lot.

My mother dives into the ocean once or
twice a day to hunt for food. Sometimes I
wait onshore with other pups. Other times, I
practice diving or napping. *Yawn* . . . I am an
all right diver, but I'm an excellent napper.
And my mother always comes back.

I'm a super sister.

I babysit my little brothers and sisters while Mmê forages for food. We play! We wrestle! I teach them how to look for food! (And I hardly ever almost never pull their hair!)

meerkat pup

My pops and me are tight!

Mi padre is cool. He watches me all the time. My half brothers and half sisters and me dash and dart. We pick and peck. Later, we will join the whole herd.

lesser rhea hatchling

Every family's different—
each family is just right!

We live in every kind of
family you can think of!

GLOSSARY

We all know that animals don't really talk! But if animals *did* talk, they certainly wouldn't all speak English. In this book, the animals occasionally use non-English words for parents. These words are commonly used in the animals' ranges, and they hint at the diversity of homelands and languages in our world.

Animal	Word	Pronunciation	Meaning	Language (and region)
White rhino	Amai	ah-MY	Mother	Shona (southern Africa)
White rhino	Baba	BAH-bah	Father	Shona (southern Africa)
Wood stork	Mi madre	mee MAY-dray	My mom	Spanish (Colombia)
Wood stork	Mis padres	mees PAH-drays	My parents	Spanish (Colombia)
Orangutan	Ibu	ee-boo	Mom	Malay (Borneo)
Elephant	Mama	MAH-mah	Mama	Swahili (Tanzania)
Elephant	Wakina mama wote	wah-KEE-nah MAH-mah WOH-tay	All the other mamas	Swahili (Tanzania)
Titi monkey	Mamãe	MAH-my	Mommy	Portuguese (Brazil)
Titi monkey	Papai	PAH-pie	Daddy	Portuguese (Brazil)
Poison dart frog	Mi p'pa	mee pah	My father	Sranan (Suriname)
Laysan albatross	Mākuahine	maah-koo-ah-HEE-nay	Mothers	Hawaiian (Hawaii)
Meerkat	Mmê	mmai	Mother	Setswana (Botswana)
Lesser rhea	Mi padre	mee PAH-dreh	Dad	Rioplatense Spanish (Argentina)

WHERE THESE ANIMALS LIVE

tundra swans: Arctic regions and parts of North America and northern Africa

raccoons: across North, Central, and South America; in several European and Asian countries

horses: almost every country in the world but not in Antarctica

pigs: all over the world except in Antarctica and far northern Arctic regions

white rhinos: southern Africa

wood storks: most South American countries, plus the southeastern tip of North America; in winter, the coasts of Central America and the southern regions of North America

beavers: throughout North America and many European and Asian countries

orangutans: the islands of Borneo and Sumatra in Southeast Asia

African elephants: thirty-seven African countries, mostly in the central and eastern parts of the continent

South American titi monkeys: several countries in South America

North American river otters: much of North America, but not the areas that are the farthest north or farthest south

green sea turtles: around the world in warm tropical and subtropical ocean waters

great white sharks: temperate (not tropical and not polar) waters around the world, especially off the coasts of North America, southern Africa, and Australia

ladybugs: all over the world except in Arctic and Antarctic regions

poison dart frogs: rain forests of Central and South America

gray wolves: mostly across the northern half of North America and parts of Asia

Laysan albatrosses: nest in northwestern Hawaiian Islands. They fly as far as Asia and North America to find food.

chinstrap penguins: on Antarctica and the subantarctic islands north of Antarctica

rhesus macaques: several countries in central and southern Asia

dogs: all over the world, except in Antarctica, where all nonnative species except humans are banned

harbor seals: coasts and coastal waters off North America, Europe, and Asia

meerkats: southern Africa

lesser rheas: southern South America

humans: across the planet

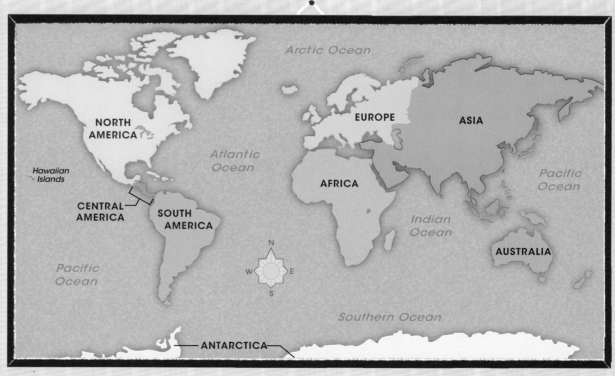

AUTHOR'S NOTE

As a kid, I devoured books and TV shows about animals. Slip-sliding otter families made me laugh, while sea turtles swimming endlessly and silently through the blue sea made me sad. Although I like time by myself, the idea of having no family seemed so lonely. But the different kinds of animal families seemed to work just fine. And sometimes, when my bossy big sisters bugged me, I thought, "Maybe sea turtles have the right idea!"

I have friends who are only children. On the other hand, my husband has seven brothers and sisters—wow! I know awesome people who grew up in all sorts of families. They were raised by adoptive parents, single parents, foster parents, or divorced parents. They lived with two moms, two dads, grandparents, other relatives, or a mom and a dad. It seems as though almost any kind of human family can be just the right kind. Basically, a family needs at least one responsible grown-up, at least one kid, and a whole lot of love.

This book celebrates all types of families. I hope peeking across the animal kingdom at different family structures will spark your interest in these animals' lives. I also hope it's a good reminder that we can be loved and cared for in many different ways.

Grateful thanks to a whole herd of professors, wildlife biologists, zoologists, translators, and native language speakers for all their thoughtful assistance. More thanks to my extended writing/book family, which includes Carol Hinz and all the Millbrook folks, my Wordsmiths critique group, and Lisa Bullard. And, always, the mother of all thank-yous to my family for their endless support.

FURTHER READING

Judge, Lita. *Born in the Wild: Baby Mammals and Their Parents.* New York: Roaring Brook, 2014.

O'Leary, Sara. *A Family Is a Family Is a Family.* Toronto: Groundwood Books, 2016.

Parr, Todd. *The Family Book.* Boston: Little, Brown, 2003.

Posada, Mia. *Guess What Is Growing inside This Egg?* Minneapolis: Millbrook Press, 2007.

Richardson, Justin, and Peter Parnell. *And Tango Makes Three.* New York: Simon & Schuster, 2005.

Rotner, Shelley, and Sheila M. Kelly. *Families.* New York: Holiday House, 2015.